1974

PROPERTY OF
SOUTH BEND COMMUNITY SCHOOL CORPORATION
ESEA II - 1974

Skyhooks

The Story of Helicopters

By the Same Author

Skyhooks

The Story of Helicopters
by Charles Coombs

3465

illustrated with 33 photographs

William Morrow and Company   New York 1967

Third printing, September 1970

Acknowledgments for Photographs

Bell Helicopter Co., 42, 71, 74, 76, 82, 83, 86
Fairchild-Hiller Corp., 61, 66, 69
Filper Research, 12
Gyrodyne Company of America, Inc., 88
Hughes Tool Co., Aircraft Division, 36, 41, 51, 53, 55, 56, 59
International Business Machines Corp., 20
Ling-Tempco-Vought, 94
Lockheed Aircraft Corporation, 91, 92
United Aircraft Corp./Sikorsky Division, 15, 17, 21, 29, 45, 49, 63, 67,
    80, 85

Table of Contents

Skyhooks

The Story of Helicopters

The Versatile Machine

Helicopters are probably the most amazing and versatile machines ever built. Small ones, with a bulging plastic canopy over the cockpit, buzz around the sky looking like oversized mosquitoes carrying light bulbs. Medium-sized ones hover overhead or dart around like hummingbirds in search of nectar. Like hawks, large ones swoop earthward, gather up heavy loads, and disappear beyond the horizon.

The helicopter is the newest vehicle, except

for spacecraft, to serve mankind. Though it is neither horse nor truck, airplane nor automobile, train nor boat, the helicopter can do the work of all of these forms of transportation.

Although at present there are definite limitations to what a helicopter can do, these limitations are being overcome as the whirlybirds increase

Small inexpensive helicopters such as this Beta 200 may one day find their way into the family garage.

in size, power, and overall efficiency. Just as jet power revolutionized travel in fixed-wing aircraft, so it has revolutionized helicopter transport.

Jet-turbine engines are immensely more advantageous than piston engines to use in helicopters. They are simpler in construction, have fewer moving parts, produce more power per pound of engine weight, and are almost foolproof. However, piston engines still are used in many small helicopters.

No other vehicle of land, sea, or sky can approach the so-called "flying eggbeater" in the variety of jobs it can do. It can take off straight up, stand still in midair, fly forward, backward, or in any direction, then land in an area the size of its own shadow. A helicopter can perform as an ambulance, a boat, a bus, a camera tripod, a car, a cowboy, or a crane. It can be used as a fan, a fire engine, a tractor, a truck, or a tugboat. It will climb mountains, explore jungles, aid law enforcement, seek and destroy enemies, or spy beneath the sea for submarines. It has a record of rescue work unparalleled in history. It is indeed a veritable "skyhook," capable of performing a limitless variety and endless number of lifting and hauling assignments.

Every day another way is found of using helicopters to perform a new task or to solve an emergency problem. Not very long ago the town of Greybull, Wyoming, was threatened with destruction. Unseasonably warm weather had caused an early breakup of ice on the Big Horn River. A massive jam of jagged ice formed in a bend, damming the stream. The water began backing up toward Greybull and the surrounding country. Roads were flooded, and surface transportation halted. Nearby ranches were threatened.

Apparently nothing could be done about the enormous jam of jumbled, dangerous ice that stretched more than a mile across the river. The cost in property could be staggering—and even some lives might be lost.

As it happened, there were two small, three-

Opposite: The massive Sikorsky S-64 aptly demonstrates the helicopter's role as a skyhook.

place Hiller 12E helicopters located in Greybull. They belonged to a small aviation firm and were normally hired out for a variety of light construction jobs or forestry work.

The helicopters were put to work around the clock, as the flood waters rose. The pilots patrolled the area, rescuing families from isolated ranches and herding livestock to the safety of high ground.

But the flooding spread, and hope faded as grinding ice packed even more solidly across the river. Then someone remembered a cache of dynamite sticks stored away for use on construction jobs. To venture onto the shifting jam in an attempt to plant the explosives in it would have been foolhardy, but the owner of the copters figured the whirlybirds might be able to accomplish what men afoot wouldn't dare attempt.

He bundled up fifty-pound charges of the dynamite, put them in gunny sacks, and weighted them with gravel to make them sink into the ice. Flying out over the ice, he explored the jam from end to end. He looked for the weakest and most

A Coast Guard helicopter rescues a hurricane survivor.

vulnerable spots in the solid pack. Then, sys-
tematically, as the chopper hovered a few feet
above the floe, an assistant heaved the charges
over the side. While the fuses burned toward
the explosives, the helicopter sped away to a safe
distance.

For twelve hours they bombed the ice jam,
using up 1,400 pounds of dynamite. Finally, the

dynamited jam gave way in a thunderous crash of grinding ice. Immediately the backed-up waters began to recede. The danger was over. The town of Greybull, surrounding ranches, and hundreds of head of livestock were saved.

This incident is just one example of the helicopter's amazing versatility.

Like Eagles' Wings

Apparently the desire to fly is part of man's nature. One can only assume that far back in prehistoric times Stone Age man envied the ability of birds to rise up from the ground and fly. How wonderful if, like a bird, he could cross above raging streams, soar to the tops of jagged mountain peaks, or speed high over thick forests. And so, down through the ages, man has attempted to develop means by which he could imitate the flight of birds.

19

Thousands of years before recorded history, legend has it, a Persian ruler gathered and trained a flock of eagles. Harnessing them to his chariot, he goaded them into flight. Wings whipped the air, but the chariot having insufficient power remained earthbound.

Centuries later the early Chinese developed lightweight spindles from which feathers set at a slight angle protruded. When twirled, these toys would lift themselves vertically into the air

Down through the ages man has attempted to imitate the ability of birds to fly.

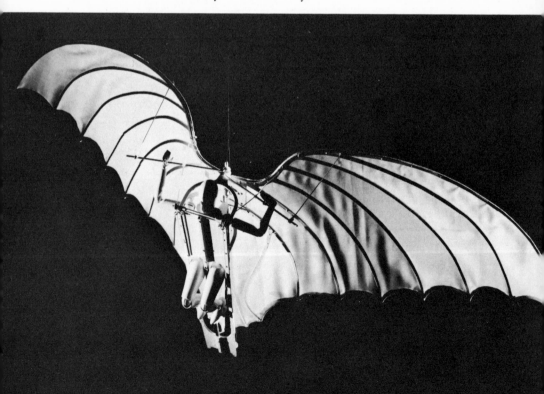

and settle back gently to earth. These "rotating wings" made use of the same theory that in time was applied successfully to helicopters.

Nearly five hundred years ago famed artist-sculptor-inventor Leonardo da Vinci designed a model of a strange contraption. It had a wing shaped like the spiral threads of an enormous screw. The reasoning behind da Vinci's design was sound. Air, he knew, had substance or density, as earth, water, wood, and infinite other

Theoretically reasonable, Leonardo da Vinci's aerial screw was a far cry from today's helicopters.

materials have substance and density. Why, then, could not a spiral wing, shaped like a screw, be made to bore itself up into the air in the same way that a metal auger bores into wood?

The experiment was certainly worth a try. But without a lightweight power source, which could rotate the spiral fast enough to generate lift, there was no chance of success.

However, da Vinci called his envisioned machine a *helixpteron* (from the Greek *helix,* meaning spiral, and *pteron,* meaning wing) and from this word eventually emerged the modern term helicopter.

Not until the present century, and the invention of the gasoline piston engine, was there enough power concentrated in a small lightweight package to start men thinking seriously again of the helicopter. Ideally, this craft had to be one that would lift itself vertically from the ground, hover in midair like a hummingbird, move in any direction, then return straight down and gently settle on the earth. Instead of vertically mounted propellers, like those used to accelerate so-called fixed-wing airplanes forward across the ground and into the sky, experimenters generally agreed that a helicopter needed horizontally mounted fans or propellers for direct upward lift.

The project involved enormous problems. A normal fixed-wing airplane takes to the air only after it has attained high speed moving across the ground. This speed is necessary so that air passes across the specially shaped wing fast enough to form slight vacuum-like eddies of air on top of the wing. Thus the pressure decreases on the upper surface of the wing, while the pressure on the underside of the wing remains strong. The imbalance of pressure, pushing upward more than downward, lifts the airplane.

Yet, if a helicopter is to take off without the benefit of forward speed, how can it acquire the necessary lift?

The answer is to spin or rotate the wings horizontally through the air without moving the entire machine. Helicopter rotors are simply thin wings shaped similarly to the wing of any ordinary airplane. By spinning vigorously, they achieve the same kind of lift that an airplane gets by speeding across the ground and into the wind.

Understanding this principle, air-minded men of many nations began trying to build these "rotary-wing" aircraft. They used the most powerful gasoline engines available. Early in the century, however, these engines were too heavy and too underpowered to turn dreams of vertical flight into reality. In France, Spain, Denmark, Germany, Austria, Italy, and elsewhere odd contraptions resembling fallen windmills appeared on vacant fields.

In 1907, Frenchman Louis Bréguet built a massive machine, which had thirty-two rotating vanes and looked like a plumber's nightmare. Yet, in a test flight, it rose some five feet off the ground. Then, for lack of proper controls, it went berserk, nearly vibrating itself to pieces. Valuing his neck, Bréguet wrestled it to the ground and never flew it again.

Not far away, another Frenchman, Paul Cornu, built an odd machine that had two rotors tipped off by blades resembling giant flyswatters. He, too, managed to get his vehicle a few feet off the ground before it began to buck, shake, and pitch. Unable to tame his flailing beast, Cornu also abandoned his project.

Then, from far-off Kiev, Russia, an eighteen-year-old lad named Igor Sikorsky set out for France to talk with Cornu and other European helicopter enthusiasts. Profiting from their errors in design, Sikorsky returned to Kiev and constructed his own craft. It had two sets of three-bladed rotors positioned one above the other.

Wisely standing aside, he started the engine. The rotors spun, straining to lift the machine. Yet, there was not sufficient power to raise it. Before shutting it off, Sikorsky also noted that the craft was unstable like the others. It tended to twist over on its side rather than to lift straight up. Stability seemed to be the major problem in any rotary-wing aircraft.

Time passed. The First World War ended. The 1920's brought renewed interest in helicopters, although no notable successes. Some could rise, but could not be controlled. There was little understanding of the many aerodynamic problems involved.

During the 1930's determined copter builders began to make real headway with vertical-lift machines. Lighter and more powerful engines became available. Trial-and-error tactics gave way to careful studies of aerodynamic problems. An older and wiser Louis Bréguet built a new whirlybird. Although underpowered, it made several successful and properly controlled flights in 1934.

In Germany, Heinrich Focke invented and built a vertical riser designated the Focke-Achgelis FW-61. The FW-61 had the fuselage of an airplane, with twin rotors stuck far out on pipe-frame outriggers. It was fully maneuverable and proceeded to break all existing records for endurance, speed, distance, and altitude. Although scarcely resembling today's rotary-wing aircraft, the Focke-Achgelis FW-61 often is considered the world's first practical helicopter.

Meanwhile, due to the Russian Revolution,

Igor Sikorsky had fled to the United States. Applying his genius to fixed-wing aircraft, he soon developed the famous Sikorsky multi-engined airplanes and flying boats. But he was still nagged by the failure of his earlier Russian-built helicopters. He gave much thought to ways of correcting their faults.

Sikorsky's employer gave him permission to continue his experimenting and set aside a corner of the factory in which he could work on his ideas. Eventually he created a welded tubular air machine. After years of work, he finished the VS-300, and on September 14, 1939, on a grassy field near Stratford, Connecticut, he tested it out.

For the test Sikorsky dressed in a warm top-coat and wore a felt hat as protection against the downwash of chill air from the spinning blades. The VS-300 had a single three-bladed main rotor, a tricycle landing gear, a complicated belt-driven transmission, and a seventy-five-horse-power air-cooled gasoline engine. It also had a small vertical-mounted, propeller-like rotor

27

perched far back on the tail. This small tail rotor, Sikorsky reasoned correctly, could be used to stabilize the craft. It would offset the tendency of most earlier single-rotor helicopters to spin in the opposite direction from the movement of the main rotor.

His co-workers watched hopefully from the sidelines as Sikorsky advanced the throttle on the VS-300. There was no telling what the vibrating contraption might do once the power was full on. No one in the United States, including Igor Sikorsky, ever had flown a helicopter. For safety precautions, the workmen had attached tether ropes to the aircraft to prevent the possibility of its soaring away out of control.

As Sikorsky continued to open the throttle, the VS-300 roared and shook as it strained against the grip of gravity. Then, suddenly, its wheels wavered off the ground. The ungainly welded-steel contraption lifted a few feet into the air, reached the end of the restraining ropes, and settled back to earth.

Igor Sikorsky smiled triumphantly. The flight

had been brief. There had been few witnesses.
The event made no big news headlines. Yet,
Sikorsky knew by the ease of that first flight, by
the relatively small amount of vibration, and by
the comforting stability of the craft, that he at
least had the basis for a helicopter that would be
of practical use to mankind.

Further flight tests, however, turned up a few
flaws in the VS-300, and a new improved version

Igor Sikorsky's VS-300 was the first
successful American helicopter.

was built. On May 13, 1940, the tether ropes were dropped and the first free flight was made. Oddly, Sikorsky found that the new VS-300 would hover or fly in any direction—except forward! After further study and careful engineering, a third model of the VS-300 was built. With each improvement, with each test flight, he gained new knowledge and confidence.

On May 6, 1941, having put a new one-hundred-horsepower engine on the craft, Sikorsky flew the VS-300 to a world helicopter endurance record of one hour, thirty-two minutes, twenty-six seconds.

Meanwhile, having closely watched the progress of the VS-300, the United States Army Air Corps asked Sikorsky to build a military test version of a similar aircraft. The first experimental copter was designated the XR-4. It was a two-seater, about twice the size of the VS-300. Instead of being constructed as an open maze of welded tubular steel, it was covered with fabric and had an enclosed cockpit. Its engine had double the horsepower of the VS-300.

After rigorous military tests, the helicopter was added to the military inventory in 1944. The "X," denoting experimental, was dropped, and Sikorsky was given an order to build more than a hundred R-4's. This contract was the first ever awarded in the United States for production of a large quantity of helicopters.

Thus, a determined Igor Sikorsky had founded the American helicopter industry.

How Do They Fly?

Learning to fly a helicopter is no more difficult than learning to operate any other fairly complicated motor vehicle. Usually experience in flying fixed-wing aircraft is helpful. This experience teaches you the basic rules of aerodynamics —what makes an aircraft fly. You become familiar with navigation and the use of various instruments. You become adept at diagnosing weather patterns and are able to evaluate other important aspects of flying. You acquire confidence in the air. These skills are fundamental to any type of flying.

Yet, there are marked differences between flying an airplane and a helicopter. For one thing, the helicopter is able to maneuver in three dimensions—forward and backward, side to side, and up and down. To learn how to handle these differences firsthand requires taking lessons. They are somewhat expensive, perhaps costing fifty dollars a flying hour. A fixed-wing pilot may need only about twenty-five additional training hours to learn rotary-wing flying and get his pilot's license certified to include helicopters. Without fixed-wing experience, an able beginner may need around forty hours to become competent.

Nor is helicopter piloting strictly a man's job. There are more than a hundred women licensed to fly helicopters in the United States, and the figure increases steadily. Many more are located in other countries. All are skilled pilots. Many of them, in fact, are helicopter instructors. As teachers, women are said to be calmer and more patient with students who find learning to fly the sensitive aircraft no easy task. Most of these women helicopter pilots belong to an international organization called The Whirly-Girls, with headquarters in Washington, D.C.

Perhaps the best way to see how a helicopter works is to get in and take a turn at the controls. You climb into the cockpit and look around. In general appearance, your surroundings are similar to those of a normal lightweight airplane. There are many familiar engine instruments—gas gauge, oil-pressure gauge, tachometer for registering engine and rotor revolutions per minute (rpm's), and so forth. Flight instruments include altimeter, compass, air-speed indicator, and the like.

You strap yourself into the seat and check the flight controls. A metal stick protrudes from near the floor and extends up between your knees. Straight or bent in a curve, it still resembles the "joystick" used in early-day light aircraft before the stick was replaced by a yoke or a steering wheel. Also, there is a pair of rudder pedals in position for your feet.

Beside your seat, within easy reach of your left hand, is another stick lying in a generally horizontal or upward slanting position. At the end of the stick is a rubber or plastic grip, which reminds you of the twist throttle on the end of motorcycle handlebars.

Assuming that you have had a lot of ground time in preparation for the flight, and perhaps have flown numerous practice missions in a ground-anchored flight simulator, you are ready to go.

You start the engine. As the engine warms up, the overhead rotor remains stationary. It certainly is different from an airplane propeller, which is geared directly to the engine shaft and always turns when the engine does. However, the helicopter rotor is a much larger and heavier mechanism, and would exert too much drag on the engine starter. As with an automobile's mechanism, a clutch or transmission device is used. The clutch engages the rotor only after the engine has been started and is properly warmed up.

Soon everything is ready. The main rotor, as

well as the small tail rotor—which is geared directly to it—are idling nicely. You are ready to take off.

You reach for the stick beside your seat. It is named the *collective pitch stick,* usually called the *collective.* Depending upon whether you want to ascend or descend, you lift or lower it to in-

Basic controls of a small helicopter—the Hughes 200.

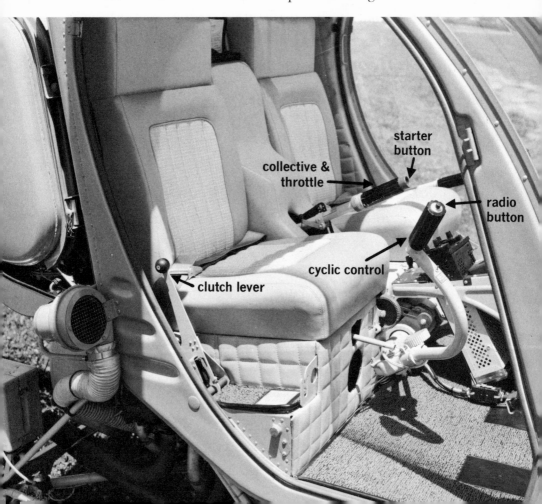

crease or decrease the amount of pitch on the rotor blades. The greater the degree of pitch, the greater the lift.

But you must also adjust the power as you adjust rotor-blade pitch. By twisting the motorcycle-like throttle on the end, you increase or decrease the rotor rpm's. Some collective sticks are coordinated so that when you lift the stick to increase the blade pitch you automatically advance the throttle.

Now you raise the collective gently and add power. The copter vibrates somewhat as the main rotor picks up speed. Dust flies as the downwash from the blades hits the ground, bounces back, and builds up a bubble, or cushion, of slightly compressed air around the chopper. This air is called *ground effect.* Ground effect aids the lift-off. You continue to exert upward pressure on the collective stick and twist the throttle for a bit more power, until the craft is airborne.

Then, after you are a few feet off the ground, the cushion of air has room to escape out the sides. Unless you add more pitch to the rotor

37

blades and twist the throttle for still more power, so that you rise above the bubble of heavy air, the copter will bounce up and down on it like a yo-yo. You control properly, however, and gain enough altitude to escape the influence of the downwash. Now you are ready to go forward, backward, or to either side.

But something strange happens when the copter starts to move in any lateral direction. On one side the blades are advancing into the wind, or rotating toward the direction of flight. On that side they generate a maximum of lift. As they circle around to the other side, however, the blades retreat away from the direction of flight, or downwind. The amount of lift decreases. Thus there is an imbalance of lift on opposite sides of the rotor arc. Unless corrected, the lift on the strong or advancing side would tip the rotor toward the weak side. The copter then would go into a violent, extremely dangerous roll.

In order to maintain balance, when moving in any direction, the blades must be adjusted each time they go around—more pitch as they retreat around the arc, less pitch as they advance. Complicated as this procedure may seem, it is a one-handed operation. You manage it with the stick that protrudes up between your knees. It is called the *cyclic pitch control,* or the *cyclic stick,* or, simpler still, the *cyclic.*

Gently, with your right hand, you move the cyclic in whatever direction you wish to go. Through a series of rods and hinges, the pitch of each rotor blade adjusts itself each time it goes around. Moving the cyclic in any direction also tilts the rotor in that direction, pulling the helicopter with it. Forward, backward, or sideways—the helicopter moves according to the pressures on the cyclic stick. Other complicated gyroscopic forces come into play and affect directional control, but guidance is generally achieved in this manner.

However, there is still the problem of torque to contend with. As the main rotor twirls in one direction, it and the engine that spins it produce a counter force pushing in the opposite direction. This reaction is explained by Sir Isaac Newton's

Third Law of Motion. Back in the seventeenth century Newton observed that for every *action* in one direction there is an equal *reaction* in the opposite direction. Release a toy balloon, and the air escaping out the nozzle in one direction (action) causes the balloon to zip around the room in the opposite direction (reaction). The kick of a gun as the bullet leaves the barrel, the lift-off of a rocket as blazing gases spurt rearward, illustrate action and reaction. Examples of the Third Law of Motion are at work all around us.

In a helicopter its operation is very noticeable. As the main rotor spins in one direction, the reaction, or torque, tends to spin the rest of the aircraft in the opposite direction. This tendency must be corrected, or the copter will pinwheel out of control.

There are several methods for correcting torque. Some copters have two main rotors that spin in opposite directions. Thus the torque from one cancels out the torque from the other. A few helicopters use small jet engines in their blade tips, or pipe hot, high-pressure gases out through

Rotor-tip vanes which eject high-pressure
gases do away with the problem of torque.

vanes in the tips, in order to spin the rotors. In
such cases the thrust is generated at the rotor
tips, not inside the aircraft. Thus the blades themselves absorb the reaction, and there is no torque
problem with which to contend.

But most helicopters do have a torque problem. The most common method for controlling it

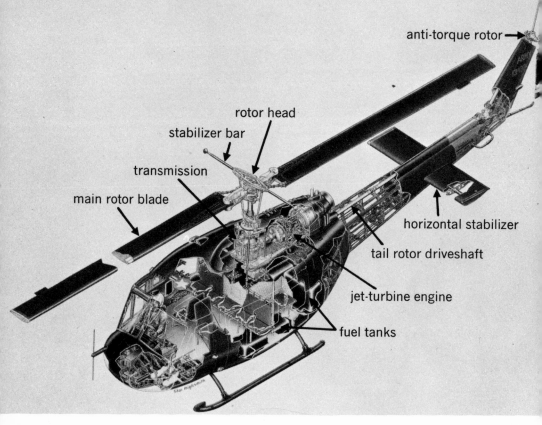

A cutaway view of a Bell UH-1 displays its basic parts.

is by the use of a small vertical tail rotor, logically called an *anti-torque rotor*.

Whether hovering or moving in any direction, you control the anti-torque rotor with the rudder pedals on the floor of the cockpit. By pushing one or the other pedal, you increase or decrease the amount of pitch in the blades of the tail rotor. In this way you either push the tail against the torque pressure or allow it to drift slightly with it. Such adjusting of the tail-rotor pitch enables you to maintain a straight course or to turn in either direction. Thus, the tail rotor not only stabilizes the copter, but serves as its rudder.

So, as you fly your helicopter, both hands and both feet are kept busy. Being a much less stable craft than an airplane, the helicopter does not allow much hands-off flying. You must coordinate your movements carefully in all maneuvers. You lift up a little on the collective to hold altitude and twist for a little extra power, as you move the cyclic gently forward to gain speed. You ease the rudder left to turn left and follow through with the cyclic stick to make a smooth turn. Actually, since the copter responds so readily, the pilot is apt to overcontrol it and go bouncing around the sky. Exerting only slight pressures on the controls is far better technique than making definite movements with them.

The one main exception occurs in the event of

43

a power failure. The helicopter has a built-in safety factor called *autorotation*. If you have been flying with the uneasy feeling that an engine failure will cause you to plunge helplessly to the ground, you needn't worry. Those rotor blades will get you safely to earth as effectively as the broad wings of an airplane. They might do it even better, since you can pick out a much smaller emergency-landing spot.

As soon as the engine quits, the transmission automatically disengages the rotor. You lower the collective stick to flatten the pitch of the rotor blades. Then you nose down into a glide. The forward momentum keeps the rotor freewheeling rapidly. The blades even pick up added rpm's as the wind fans through them. Despite the flat pitch of the blades, the turning of the rotor provides a sufficient amount of lift to stretch your glide toward a landing spot—but not enough to prevent a crash. There is one more thing to do.

Opposite: The main rotor heads on some
helicopters are very complicated mechanisms.

Just before you reach the ground, you pull up firmly on the collective stick. This action puts full pitch back into the windmilling blades. For a few seconds lift returns. At least, enough lift to break the fall. You pull back on the cyclic stick, flare out, tail down, and settle gently to the ground.

You take a deep breath, thankful for the thing called autorotation. You have flown a helicopter. The experience was not as difficult as you had expected, not as easy as you had hoped.

But there is nothing quite like it!

Air Taxis

Surface travel is becoming more crowded and difficult every day. More people want to go more places. As a result, there are more automobiles, buses, trucks, ships, airplanes, and every other type of transportation.

In turn, congestion increases. Roads become clogged, and traffic often comes to a standstill. Although waterways may be less crowded, travel by water is slow. Airlines offer the fastest travel, but the airports, which need space for their long

47

runways, invariably are quite a distance from civic centers. The air passenger on a short trip of a few hundred miles may take more time to get back and forth to the airport than to make the actual flight.

The helicopter is able to avoid this congestion by leapfrogging over it. For this reason, a growing number of cities now operate helicopter airlines and heliports. Nearly all large airline terminals offer helicopter services to shuttle airline passengers back and forth to nearby cities in order to make quick connections with jet airliners. Sometimes the fare to use the copter is little more than a taxi fare would be over the same distance. The time saved often is worth much more than the cost involved.

A pioneer in this type of airport-to-midtown service is New York Airways. Depending upon traffic conditions, the ground taxi trip to or from John F. Kennedy International Airport and downtown Manhattan takes around half an hour. The Boeing-Vertol copter makes the trip from the heliport atop the Pan-Am Building to the airport

A Sikorsky S-61 awaits its passengers
at the Los Angeles International Airport.

in about seven comfortable and breathtakingly
scenic minutes. Los Angeles, San Francisco, Chi-
cago, Boston, and many other major cities have

49

similar types of helicopter service. When traffic warrants, large "sky bus" helicopters, such as the twenty-eight-passenger Sikorsky S-61 or the sixty-seven-passenger S-65, are used.

Usually there is a network of heliports surrounding a large city. Thus, the passenger can be dropped off or picked up at the one nearest his home or business.

But helicopter operations certainly are not confined to major metropolitan areas and their nearby airports. Many moderate-sized and most small cities lack airport facilities to handle normal airline traffic. Yet the need for rapid transit can be as critical in a small city or town as in a large one. The helicopter, large or small, makes an excellent short- to medium-range feeder-line vehicle. It can gather up passengers, mail, or merchandise in widespread communities and rush them to large metropolitan airports. There, with a minimum loss of time, passengers and cargo are transferred to high-speed fixed-wing airliners for the long-distance leg of the journey.

For these smaller operations, the size and

number of copters used is scaled down to fit the work and passenger load. These heli-taxi operators, in increasing numbers, are scattered around the country. Generally, they use the smaller types of copters, such as the Bell three-passenger Ranger, the Hughes Model 300, or even the two-place Brantly Model B2B. The larger, faster, turbine-powered Bell Jet Ranger, Hughes 500, and Hiller 1100 are even more ideally suited to short-range

The Hughes 500 executive helicopter
helps businessmen make their rounds at speeds
of 150 mph within a range of 450 miles.

heli-taxi operations tying outlying rural areas to metropolitan complexes. Thus the helicopter makes commuting or deliveries between moderately distant communities faster and more convenient.

Many business firms and corporations find that owning their own helicopter, sometimes several of them, is advantageous. In business, where time is money, executives can get where they're going much quicker by whirlybirding between plants or to and from the airport. Operators of offshore oil wells use helicopters almost exclusively to shuttle workers and critical supplies back and forth to isolated drill rigs.

Quite a number of helicopters are owned and used by private citizens. Most use them for both business and pleasure, just as fixed-wing pilots often use their light planes for weekday work and weekend fun. Whatever the purpose, the light helicopter excels in reaching otherwise inaccessible places. It doesn't need a prepared pad from which to operate. A parking lot, a lawn, a sandbar in the middle of a stream, a frozen lake, a weedy

Light helicopters are convenient
for many leisure activities.

field—virtually any clear area about forty feet
across serves as a handy heliport for small, vertical rising and descending copters. Add a pair of
pontoons, and any swamp or puddle-sized body
of water also becomes a helipad.

Its versatility makes the helicopter an excellent vehicle for use in police work and rescue missions.

Police officers in Lakewood, California, for example, maintain a round-the-clock helicopter patrol. As a result, they are never more than two and a half minutes away from the scene of any crime committed in the Los Angeles suburb.

The helicopters used are Hughes 300's. They are fitted with a radio, a camera, an 8,000-watt portable searchlight for night use, and other police gear. From their cruising vantage points above the community of about 100,000 inhabitants, the "copter cops" keep the entire community under protective vigilance. Radio contact and special signal lights enable them to keep in constant communication with police patrol cars.

"We believe it is virtually impossible for a suspect to escape from the scene of any crime," the Lakewood mayor asserts. "The helicopters

Opposite: Copter cops and patrol-car officers team up for effective police coverage.

can trail a suspect, hover above him, and direct ground patrols to his capture. If necessary, the copter police may land and take part in apprehending the suspect."

The Lakewood experiment with copter patrols is a test case, the first in the country. If successful, helicopters may become increasingly important in police work. In many crowded parts of the country, copters are used for traffic control. They quickly spot traffic snarls and accidents.

Helicopters such as these Hughes 300's have become important in highway traffic control.

Some cities with traffic problems have set up airwatch systems. When serious highway congestion is spotted by the copter patrolman, he radios his report to the police communications center. He also suggests alternate routes motorists may take in order to avoid a traffic jam. The traffic warning as well as the recommended alternate routes are relayed to radio stations. The station announcer or disc jockey interrupts his program to pass the message on to the motorist driving along listening to his car radio.

In case of accidents, the copter police officer will help bring care to the injured. He will radio for an ambulance and also call for a tow truck to clear the wreckage from the road. If necessary, he may land and provide emergency aerial ambulance service for the injured.

Police helicopters help prevent accidents by patrolling along high-speed highways. The sight or sound of such a helicopter usually is enough to slow down most speeders. If a speeder doesn't respond, the copter pilot radios a police patrol car. Immediately the patrol car with a flashing red light or a wailing siren arrives to pull over the reckless driver.

Helicopters frequently perform rescue work. This rescue work often is in the form of aerial ambulance service. Thousands of lives have been saved by using helicopters to rush critically ill or injured patients to a hospital. An increasing number of hospitals are installing heliports in order to save time.

A hospital heliport need not involve elaborate arrangements. A patch of concrete or grass will serve the purpose. There should be at least a beacon light for night use, and a radio hookup with the helicopter in order that the staff can be forewarned and ready to receive an emergency patient. The helicopter pad should be located as near as possible to the hospital's emergency entrance, so there will be no undue delay in getting the person quickly cared for.

In addition to the accomplishments of the aerial ambulance services, copters have saved thousands of other lives by going out on emergency rescue missions. Nearly everyone has

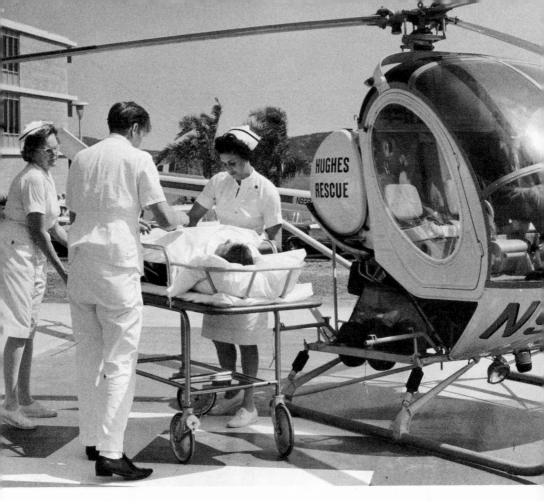

A Hughes 300 copter rushes an
emergency patient to the hospital.

heard of the heroic efforts of the chopper pilots
in these dramatic and often much-publicized in-
cidents.

In a driving December storm, the lumber ship

Alaska Cedar with a crew of twenty-four aboard lost power and ran aground on the rocky coast near Coos Bay, Oregon. Immediately the ship began to break up. The deck was soon awash, a shambles of crashing loose lumber and swirling water. Several of the crew were injured. Although the rocky shore was nearby, the raging sea prevented the crewmen from reaching it. Ship and crew seemed doomed.

Not far away James C. Klotz, a copter pilot for a construction company, was even then battling the wind as he airlifted some eight-hundred-pound sections of pipe with his Hiller 12E copter. Notified of the stricken ship, he dropped the pipe and hurried out to lend a hand.

Bucking into the howling winds, Klotz managed to reach the ship. But he found the rolling deck cluttered with guy lines, masts, crane booms, and loose timber. To land on the ship was impossible. Groping for a solution, Klotz flew back to the mainland and picked up a thin rope.

Once again over the doomed ship, he hovered low and dropped one end of the light line to one

Along the storm-tossed Oregon coast a copter
pilot rigs a lifeline to a doomed ship.

of the beleaguered seamen. In the howling mael-
strom no verbal directions were possible, but
they were not needed. The crewman tied the end
of a heavy ship's hawser to the thin line lowered
from the hovering helicopter. But before Klotz
could start shoreward with it, a wall of churning
surf engulfed his machine. Witnesses saw the
helicopter completely disappear in the foaming

white water and figured that Jim Klotz had made his last flight. Yet, somehow, the chopper managed to shake itself free of the sea's grasp.

Quickly, Klotz hauled the light line and the heavy hawser shoreward. He landed among the boulders and anchored the big line around some rocks. Thus he had rigged a lifeline from ship to shore. The injured mariners were the first to reach safety on the quickly assembled breeches buoy. As more help arrived, Klotz left and flew the stricken sailors to a United States Coast Guard station for emergency medical aid. Meanwhile, the rest of the crew made the shore just before the *Alaska Cedar* broke up and sank in the raging sea.

The saving of the crew of the *Alaska Cedar* is typical of the many and varied rescue operations performed by helicopters. When American astronauts prepare to blast off from Cape Kennedy on a space mission, their survival, too, may depend

Opposite: A helicopter plucks an astronaut
safely from the sea on his return from a flight.

on any of the several helicopters hovering off-shore from the launch pads. If something should go wrong during lift-off, the astronauts are trained to fire their rocket escape hatch, which will parachute them into the sea. There whirlybirds will be standing by ready to pluck the men out of the water.

Also, as they return to earth after a successful mission in space, the astronauts depend on one or more helicopters standing by for the splashdown. They rely on the choppers not only to find them, but to lift them up and place them on the solid deck of a recovery ship.

Indeed, in more ways than can be easily counted, helicopters have become the flying carpets of the twentieth century.

Working Whirlybirds

Helicopters, the universal skyhooks, have been put to widespread use in both industry and agriculture. Perhaps one of the most dramatic industrial uses of the modern whirlybirds is the setting up of new power lines to answer the ever-growing demands for more electricity.

The terrain of the proposed route of a new line may consist of dense woods, steep canyons, or other natural obstacles. It may be so rugged that survey teams cannot get through it without great difficulty. In some cases they may be denied access to the right of way. A helicopter is called in at once. It carries a survey team out over the wilderness, sets men and equipment down on isolated peaks, narrow ledges, or small forest clearings. If the clearing is not there, a man and chain saw can be lowered by cable from the helicopter to hack out a temporary helipad. By leapfrogging from one location to another, the surveyors travel

Helicopters transport survey or construction parties to the most difficult sites.

along the route and work out a plan for the power line.

Once the locations are established, the copter begins shuttling workmen and materials to set up the poles or to build power-line towers. When constructing towers, the choppers first hover over prepared holes in dirt or rock, dangling drums of wet concrete, and pour the footings.

Then comes the steel or aluminum. Tons of it.

Power-line tower riggers shuttle back and forth to work in a Sikorsky S-58 helicopter.

Often entire prefabricated sections of the tower are toted through the air. After delivery, they are carefully bolted into place by skilled riggers. As the tower reaches ever higher into the sky, the copter saves the riggers a laborious climb to the top. It picks them up and deposits them by hovering gently over the tower or perhaps by resting a skid or wheel on a tower beam. From that position the riggers climb out and go back to work. Obviously this maneuver takes real skill and an observance of safety precautions.

When the towers are complete, the next job is to hang the insulators and string the wires. Normally this procedure takes a large crew of men many days, working slowly under difficult and treacherous conditions.

The helicopter greatly simplifies the operation. It takes hold of one end of the cable and strings it along the line of towers. If the cable is a particularly large and heavy one, the copter first strings a light plastic or hemp pilot line, or "sock line." The main wires are then attached to the pilot line and pulled through from the ground.

Often, when poles instead of towers are used, the copters transport the crews to dig the holes. Then they fly back, put a sling around a pole, and carry it to the prepared site. One by one the poles are lowered into their holes. Then, with poles set, the copters string the cables in a fraction of the time that the job takes when done manually.

Even after the lines are in operation, the helicopter has a job of patrolling and inspecting

A helicopter strings a transmission line in a
fraction of the time required by a ground crew.

them. This method is a vast improvement over the old one of an inspector plodding along on foot or horseback. Staring up against the bright sky looking for frayed wires, cracked or scorched insulators, bird's nests, or fallen branches was never satisfactory. Now the chopper skims along close to the wires, giving the inspector a much better view. In this way a copter team can patrol some eight hundred miles of power line a week, while a man afoot or on horseback could cover only about forty miles.

In severe winter conditions, the weight of heavy ice collecting on wires sometimes threatens to topple poles or break power or telephone lines. Helicopters have been called on to fly along slowly just above the wires. The downwash of air from the rotors, plus the sound vibrations, cracks and shakes the ice from the wires.

Within the limits of range and lifting power, there are few jobs not suited to the versatile

Opposite: Power lines are inspected quickly and efficiently with a helicopter.

70

whirlybird. What can't be carried inside the copter usually can be dangled outside. For example, helicopters are sometimes used as a flying camera tripod. When the idea was first tried, the copter's inherent rotor vibration made the aerial movies jumpy and fuzzy. Then, in Hollywood, a young man named Nelson Tyler devised a cushioned and counterweighted stable platform that holds the camera steady despite the helicopter's jiggling and maneuvering.

As the result of the Tyler Camera System, airborne cameramen are in demand. Their work is quickly recognizable. Any time you view a scene from overhead—even slightly above ground level —and wonder how in the world it could have been photographed, chances are it was taken from a helicopter. Movie chase or battle scenes, deer stampeding along a mountain ridge, a distant tiny patch of blue evolving slowly and steadily into a swimming pool complete with bathers, these and myriad other scenes are filmed from helicopters. Television commercials of all kinds are written around the helicopter's ability to follow the action

72

from angles that would be otherwise quite impossible. For instance, following an automobile from a distance as it winds and twists along a mountain road, or a man on horseback galloping through a grape vineyard, are well-known examples of television commercials shot from helicopters.

The government and the National Aeronautics and Space Administration use airborne cameras for filming various surveys and space programs. Indeed, helicopters have added a whole new dimension to movie making. Their use is certain to increase, and the results may well become even more amazing.

The helicopter repeatedly proves its worth in fighting forest fires. As soon as a new blaze is spotted, the nearest available helicopters are called in. By the time trained heli-jumpers are ready to go, the copters arrive to whisk them quickly to the location of the new smoke. Arriving at the fire, if a nearby clearing is available, a copter sets the fire fighters on the ground. If landing is not feasible, the helicopter soars to a safe altitude from which the heli-jumpers can use their parachutes. In either case, the helicopter provides the essential speed in getting equipment and fire fighters to the scene of a new blaze.

In addition, the helicopter functions effectively as an aerial fire truck. It can spill tankloads of fire retardant directly onto or in front of an advancing blaze. At times, skilled helicopter pilots have been able to control the movement of flames by hovering nearby and directing the rotor down-wash against the fire.

In less than a minute a Bell 47 helicopter lays more fire hose than a ground crew can manage in a half hour.

Helicopters are used to lay fire hose across wooded areas that would be infinitely more difficult and time consuming to penetrate on foot. Above all, helicopters are used to rescue fire fighters who may get trapped by the terrain or threatened by a quick change in the direction of a fire's movement.

If a woodland has been devastated, helicopters can take on the work of reforestation. In denuded areas, rank weeds usually spring up first and blanket young forest seedlings from needed sunlight. Helicopters spray weed killers, which affect only the weeds. They wither and die, leaving the young trees sunlight and headroom in which to grow.

In logged-off areas, tree seeds are also sown by helicopters in order to maintain a continuing growth of timber.

Helicopters often move in to sow fast-growing cover crops, such as mustard or rye, in the wake of hillside brush fires. The seeds root quickly and keep the topsoil from being washed away by winter rains before lasting growth returns.

In no area is the helicopter more widely used, or more valuable, than in agriculture. The most important operation in this work, known generally as "ag flying," is crop dusting and spraying. A helicopter can spray many acres of cotton, tomatoes, corn, or other crops in a single minute. Orchards can be sprayed quickly against pests, and fruit crops saved. The downwash from the rotors bounces off the ground, producing a "boiling effect." This churning air distributes the spray or dust on the underside of the foliage as well as on top.

Spraying or dusting by helicopter is an
enormously successful method of pest control.

Copters play their part in agricultural fertilizing and seeding, although they are not generally used for these purposes in farming. They are, however, widely used to spread herbicides for killing noxious weeds that threaten crops or encroach on fields along fence lines.

Cotton harvests have been improved by spraying defoliation chemicals from helicopters and removing the leaves before the pickers go to work.

Helicopters sometimes answer emergency calls to save a crop threatened by some unexpected whim of nature. Sudden low temperatures in a citrus grove, a cherry orchard, or a tomato field may set off an alert to the whirlybird "frost patrol." Due to an inversion, the freezing air may lie close to the ground, while a few feet higher up the air may be nearly five degrees warmer. By flying back and forth above the field, the helicopter rotors fan the warmer air down so that it displaces the frostier air threatening fruit or vegetables.

On occasion, untimely rains soak ripening

fruit such as cherries, peaches, figs, or apricots. Normally, such crops would be water spotted, rotted, and otherwise ruined. Helicopters, however, can be called in to cruise above the water-soaked crop, their downwash knocking off the harmful droplets. Even if a bit of fruit is shaken loose, the major crop is salvaged. On the other hand, in some places, copters have been used deliberately to blow pecans and walnuts off trees in order that they can be easily gathered up for the harvest.

Ranchers use the maneuverable choppers to herd cattle, or chase them out of deep arroyos or dense underbrush for cowboys to herd. Helicopters also enable ranchers to patrol and repair fence lines quickly.

Indeed, in many ways the helicopter has become an indispensable servant to man. As new chores and new problems arise, the helicopter will become even more of a universal skyhook.

Birds of War

Until the early 1950's rotary-wing aircraft were few in number. Little practical use had been made of them. Like nervous nestlings, they had been testing their wings.

Then helicopters came of age during the war in Korea. The terrain there was rugged and often muddy, bogging down machines and troops alike. More and more, helicopters were called upon to carry supplies to forward positions. They helped lay communication lines across impenetrable swamps and forests. Piece by piece they lifted pontoon bridges into place. They hauled troops and ammunition and flew reconnaissance missions to spot enemy movements.

Copters rescued downed pilots and evacuated wounded soldiers. Often under intense enemy fire, they airlifted trapped units to safe ground. An estimated 25,000 lives were saved by helicopters during the Korean War.

As a result, after the war ended, all branches of the military service became intensely inter-

A downed pilot is lifted to safety by an
Aerospace Rescue and Recovery Service helicopter.

ested in how they might utilize helicopters. The United States government was willing to appropriate substantial sums of money to encourage manufacturers to develop new and improved rotary-wing machines. Helicopters grew in size, in speed, and in safety. Jet-turbine engines were introduced, and now they have replaced the heavier and less powerful piston-engines in most copters.

During the cold war, and later in far-off Vietnam, the army and marines began to experiment with heliborne units. Tactics based on the movement of entire companies of troops by swarms of helicopters were developed. Assault copters that could carry anywhere from a half dozen to around fifty fully equipped men were built by Bell, Sikorsky, and Boeing-Vertol.

By the time American troops began fighting in Vietnam, large-scale helicopter warfare was a definite military plan, if not a battle-tested fact.

Success and survival in war depend largely upon the mobility of men and supplies. There are few roads in Vietnam, and most of them are controlled by Communist forces. Impenetrable jungles, swift rivers, and rugged mountains make the movement of troops and supplies by ground both difficult and hazardous. The lack of suitable airstrips severely limits troop movement by fixed-wing aircraft. Only the helicopter adapts itself properly to the job.

From the Mekong Delta in the south to Da Nang in the north, heliborne units wage a steady war against the infiltrating Vietcong. The first and perhaps the best known of these units is the United States First Cavalry Division (Airmobile). When a heliborne assault is called, swarms of choppers belonging to the First Cav load up with combat-ready troops. The shriek of turbine en-

An armed helicopter "gunship" strafes the battle area prior to a heliborne troop landing.

gines and the thumping of rotors announce their departure as they head for the attack area. The men huddle anxiously inside while the copter pilots fly just high enough to stay out of range of sniping Vietcong ground fire.

But before the troop-carrying choppers arrive at the landing zone, special rocket-toting, machine-gun-firing "gunships" swoop in and rake the area thoroughly. The concerted firepower drives the enemy into their tunnels or at least "keeps their heads down" for a while. The gunships constantly change their direction of attack to confuse enemy defenses. With the Vietcong pinned down and confused, the troop-carrying copters swoop in quickly and unload. Then they

Combat-ready troops are brought swiftly
to the battlefield by helicopter.

get out again before the Communist infiltrators can recover sufficiently to train their weapons on either the whirlybirds or the freshly landed troops. Although somewhat vulnerable to ground fire, the retreating helicopters dodge low along the treetops or rice paddies, offering difficult targets at best.

Meanwhile, the armed gunships such as the Bell UH-1 "Hueys," or the newer, faster, and much more lethally armed attack helicopters—with the technical designation of Advanced Aerial Fire Support System (AAFSS)—continue orbiting the area and firing upon enemy positions.

Thus a search-and-destroy mission can be heliborne to any area in a matter of minutes without alerting the enemy. When the strike is finished, and the smoke of battle has cleared, the choppers swoop back down to pick up the troops, move them to a new position, or return them to their home base.

Opposite: A Sikorsky CH-54A Army Skycrane hauls a 6½-ton howitzer to battle.

Thus, the famous Bell "Hueys," the Boeing-Vertol "Chinooks," and several models of large Sikorsky helicopters launch the attacks and supply the troops with the essentials of survival in the airmobile war.

These same helicopters are used to evacuate refugees, airlift field artillery pieces, and serve in many other capacities.

In Vietnam, as in Korea, the most important job the helicopters perform is saving lives.

Helicopter ambulances rush the wounded to medical aid.

Search and rescue of marooned troops or downed pilots go on constantly. A special unit called the Aerospace Rescue and Recovery Service (ARRS) does the large share of this duty. 'The Jolly Green Giant' is the affectionate name given to the mottled-green camouflaged rescue copters. But any helicopter at any time will peel off quickly and go to the aid of anyone in distress.

Serving as airborne ambulances, the copters are peerless machines of mercy. No wounded soldier is more than a few minutes away from medical care.

Navy helicopters also have important functions to carry out, including search-and-rescue work. No fixed-wing pilot takes off from a carrier deck, or returns to it later, without the comforting knowledge that helicopters are hovering nearby to snatch him from the water if he is forced to crash-land into the sea.

Seaborne helicopters conduct anti-submarine warfare (ASW). The self-homing torpedoes they carry can be directed to undersea targets by assorted detection instruments aboard their mother ship. Or the copters can be equipped with their own sonar sound-detecting apparatus, which they dip into the sea to sniff out marauders. Once located, the sub becomes easy prey of the torpedoes.

In some cases, pilotless, guided, drone anti-submarine helicopters (DASH) are launched from shipboard. When aloft, they drop their explosive sub-seeking bombs upon the unsuspecting quarry.

Navy helicopters have been used on occasion as mine sweepers, dragging hooks or cables through the water to uproot dangerous explosives.

In war as well as in peace, the helicopter has become an essential and versatile machine.

A pilotless drone anti-submarine helicopter (DASH) drops its pair of self-homing, sub-seeking torpedoes.

In the Crystal Ball

For many years there has been talk of the day when every backyard will be a helipad and every garage will hold a family helicopter. That day may be slow in coming. Private "helicars" might help ease highway congestion, but at the same time they might cause congestion in the sky. Also, even the most friendly neighbors would be disturbed by a helicopter landing or taking off next door, rattling windows, filling the air with dust, and assaulting the eardrums.

Still, small one-man heli-scooters are being made and experimented with. Although they are now of primary interest to the military, if found to be safe and practical, they may one day find their way into the family garage.

Today, however, more stress is being put on bigger helicopters, which are being built to carry heavier loads and more passengers over greater distances at faster speeds. Systems are being designed in which the helicopter is strictly a power unit. It will hook onto a preloaded cargo container, or a special type of bus-van, and carry it to some distant destination.

But a helicopter has drawbacks. Its range is generally short. Its forward speed is limited largely by the strain put upon the rotors and by so-called "rotor stall," which occurs when the blades lose their lift as they swing rearward, in opposite direction to the vehicle's velocity. There are still other complicated technical problems that cut down on the advantages of using a helicopter over a fixed-wing airplane.

The answer, of course, is to combine the better

A compound helicopter has short wings and a
forward-thrusting engine in addition to its rotors.

qualities of the helicopter and the fixed-wing airplane into one composite vehicle. This approach
can be seen in the so-called V/STOLS, or Vertical and Short Takeoff and Landing aircraft. In
other words, add wings to a helicopter to help
keep it aloft and give it a separate power source
for extra forward speed.

Such experimental aircraft are already flying.

They are called compound helicopters. Once airborne, the auxiliary engines on these machines send them speeding forward, and the usually small, added wings take much of the lifting job off the rotors. Some helicopters of this type are

Lockheed's proposed compound helicopter takes off vertically, folds and stows its rotor blades, and becomes a 500 mph jet airplane.

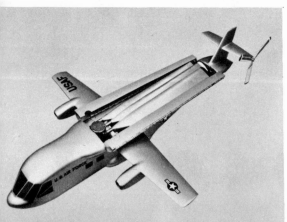

being so designed that they can fold their rotors in flight and stow them away, converting the helicopter into a fixed-wing craft. There are many proposed methods for crossbreeding helicopters and airplanes. Some of the resulting machines are called convertiplanes.

One such convertiplane, which has flown with considerable success, is the Ling-Temco-Vought XC-142A. This one is of the tilt-wing variety. During takeoff and landing, the wing and the four engines attached to it tilt vertically. Thus, the propellers act in similar fashion to a helicopter's main rotor. Once airborne, the wing and the engines swivel to a normal horizontal position. Presto, the helicopter becomes an airplane with an airplane's added speed and range.

There are several other types of convertiplanes. Some use propellers, some ducted fans that divert the thrust in any direction, and some swivel only the engines.

Certainly we can look forward to the day when giant heli-buses will take off from convenient downtown heliports, change themselves into

A composite photo shows the tilt-wing
XC-142A in its four attitudes of flight.

high-speed jet airplanes, streak across the country at supersonic velocities, and land gently again
on some distant metropolitan helipad.

Meanwhile, the fast-developing science of vertical airlift vehicles—be they helicopters, tilt
wings, convertiplanes of other design, or whatever—offers great promise for the future.

A big part of that future hovers overhead in
the sky!

Index

indicates illustration

95